Won By One

Wendy Treat

Published by
Christian Faith Center
and
Casey Treat Ministries
PO Box 98800
Seattle, WA 98198

Won By One
ISBN 978-0-931697-61-6
Copyright 1986 Wendy Louise Treat
Printed in USA 1986
Second Printing 1992
Third Printing 2009
All rights reserved
Published by Casey Treat™ Ministries
P.O. Box 98800
Seattle, Washington 98198

Special Thanks:
Tasha Treat and Terry Schurman, Editors
Megidos.com, Photography
JakStudios, Cover Art
Lisa Garrison, Cover design

Table of Contents

Forward

Preface

This book will fill a great need and be a tremendous help to so many new Christians who sincerely want to learn how to follow Jesus. They will learn how to be His representative, how to receive His power, and most of all, how to effectively witness about Jesus Christ and lead others to the new birth.

You have really covered the subject and presented your ideas in ordinary language that will be understood by the many who are seeking for this instruction and knowledge.

May God make your book a blessing to innumerable people, so that you will realize the fulfillment of your dream to help them by sharing what you have learned in such a practical way.

T.L. Osborn

Pastors Casey and Wendy Treat

Forward

I'm excited that you've received a copy of *Won By One*. Thousands of people who have heard this message from Wendy have had their lives greatly affected. I know your life will be affected, too. Since 1980, we have had the awesome experience of watching Christian Faith Center grow from 30 to over 10,000 people. Each year, thousands of men and women have been and continue to be born again and filled with the Holy Spirit in our services, and much of the fruit of this ministry comes to pass because of Wendy and the people she has trained.

As you read the following pages, I pray the anointing of the Holy Spirit that has caused thousands to be born again and filled with the Holy Spirit at CFC will come into your life, and bring you to an exciting new realm of Christian ministry.

Casey Treat

Preface

My heart's desire is to see people born again and filled with the Holy Spirit. I want to see people learn how to minister to the lost and hurting in an anointed, effective, and confident way. In order to win our world for Jesus, we need to know what we are doing and why we are doing it.

I was born again when I was 17 years old. Right away I desired for people to know Jesus and His power in their lives. I struggled with being insecure and often did not know what to do or how to effectively help people know Jesus. I was intimidated by almost every situation that I was presented with. The people I witnessed to were older or younger, richer or poorer than I was. The devil was using every way he could to try to keep me quiet.

I went through many evangelism classes and came out more insecure than before. Most of the classes were so complicated that I just knew I could never learn it, let alone share it with someone else. I would go street witnessing and be afraid to approach people. I truly believed I wouldn't know what to say, even if they did want to listen to me. Not knowing what to say or what to do can really lower your confidence level and take away your boldness.

Casey and I started Christian Faith Center in 1980, and as the Word was taught we quickly saw that signs were following. People were coming to receive from God and we needed to know how to help them receive what they were looking for. As we began researching and studying scripture we determined to find a simple, scripturally based teaching to help minister to those seeking a relationship with Him.

What you will find in this book are the results of that searching and giving of ourselves to learn God's ways. His ways are always simple, clear, and easy. This book is not a man's plan or another "program," but straight teaching from God's Word about how you can help a person be born again and filled with the Holy Spirit. It is God's Word that produces results in people's lives. Although they can be good at times, emotional experiences, your testimony, or what you have heard from other people will not produce fruit for God's Kingdom. God's Word will remain, and will produce lasting results.

In this book, I am sharing with you what I have learned over the years from training thousands of people to be able ministers of God's Word. These people have individually helped thousands of others to be born again and filled with the Holy Spirit.

I believe that if you will apply faith to the knowledge you receive from this book, and act on it, you will see tremendous results. There is nothing more joyous and fulfilling than helping a person be born again or filled with the Holy Spirit. You are an able minister and you can do it!

Won By One: as each one of us reaches out to one, we will change one life; that one will change another, and the cycle will continue until the world knows Jesus! I believe God will open the eyes of your understanding as you read these pages, and that the spirit and life of these words will become a reality in your life.

Wendy

Wendy Treat

1
Laborers Together
in His Harvest

"The harvest truly is plentiful, but the laborers are few. Therefore pray the Lord of the harvest to send out laborers into His harvest." Matthew 9:37, 38

Jesus tells us that the harvest is ready and people are anxiously waiting to hear the good news of Jesus Christ. The moment you became a Christian, you became one of His laborers in gathering His harvest and spreading the message of salvation. Christians all over the world are praying what Jesus exclaimed in Matthew 9:38, that there might be laborers sent into His harvest. Your desire to reach others for Christ is the result of those prayers and the stirring of the Holy Spirit that is within you.

Having the desire to lead people to Jesus is the first step in ministering to the needs of other people, but it is only the first step and you must continue on from there. The second step is learning how to effectively get someone born again and filled with the Holy Spirit. The fact that you are reading this book shows that you have that desire and you are now seeking for the knowledge, understanding, and confidence taught in the Bible.

> *"And Jesus came and spoke to them, saying, 'All authority has been given to Me in heaven and on earth. Go therefore and make disciples of all nations, baptizing them in the name of the Father and of the Son and of the Holy Spirit, teaching them to observe all things that I have commanded you; and lo, I am with you always, even to the end of the age.' Amen." Matthew 28:18-20*

In Verse 19, Jesus says, "Go therefore and make disciples." He does not offer us an alternative option. Nor does He say, "All who are pastors" or "All who have the time." No! He says, "Go therefore..." That is a commandment God has given to all Christians. As He was ascending into Heaven, Jesus did not recommend that we try to chat with as many people as we can about Him. No, He said, "Go!" and that commandment was given to every Christian.

There is a promise with His command to "Go". Jesus said in verse 20, "and lo, I am with you always..." This is the greatest news yet. He is with you always; the source of every good thing is inside of you! God did not command you to do something and leave you on your own to figure out the way to accomplish it. When you are born again and filled with the Holy Spirit, God is in you and working with you. In Zechariah 4:6b it says, "Not by might, nor by power, but by my Spirit, says the Lord of hosts." When you step out in faith to witness, you are relying on God's strength and His Spirit to enable you.

Jesus says in Acts 1:8, "But you shall receive power when the Holy Spirit has come upon you; and you shall be witnesses to Me in Jerusalem, and in all Judea and Samaria, and to the end of the earth." If you have been filled with the Holy Spirit, you have His power at your disposal to be used for specific reasons—one is to witness. Once you are filled with the Holy Spirit, you are to go into all the world and make disciples. You are to witness to all people and bring them into the kingdom of God. This job was not designated to a few select radicals, it was given to every Christian and therefore we cannot relent with the expectation that someone else will do it for us. The commandment has been given to all and the power is within us!

Throughout denominational churches and religious organizations, the body of Christ has often lacked knowledge and teaching of how to get someone saved and/or filled with the Holy Spirit. As a result, people are afraid to speak up and feel that due to their lack of knowledge they would never be able to do it. The devil has used that lack of knowledge as a tool to silence the church and strip us of our duties as Christians to stand strong and loudly proclaim the good news of Jesus Christ.

Thank God for His Word and the knowledge that we can find therein. We are finding out that helping someone else be born again and filled with the Holy Spirit is clearly laid out for us in His Word. The concept was established by God and as His able ministers we are equipped by Him to carry out His mission. His Word makes it very easy for us to reach people and makes helping others one of the greatest joys of being saved.

We, the Body of Christ, need every single person to say, "I recognize the high calling I have in this area. I recognize the importance of my decision to give of myself to bring people to Christ". We must see it as our highest calling. It is the most important part of our lives—emptying hell and filling heaven. The gift of eternal life is the greatest gift you can give someone. Take a moment to think about the importance of the task set before you. Before you proceed to the following pages, decide that you are willing to do what God has enabled and commanded you to accomplish.

2
Preparing to Minister

God has entrusted to you the care of newborn members of His family. Although it may seem to be overwhelming, it is not an impossible task. As you prepare, discipline, and train yourself, God will bring people to you for you to minister to. If you are faithful to walk in His Word, pray, and minister His love boldly, God will make sure that the seed you have planted into someone's life will not be destroyed or stolen. God will bless you and the people you minister to, and He will use you far beyond what you can even imagine.

As an able minister of the gospel, you need to know how to effectively minister God's Word to all people so they will not only receive salvation and the baptism of the Holy Spirit, but they will be firmly grounded in the Word of God. Knowledge of God's Word will allow new Christians to understand what they have and will give them a strength that the devil cannot take from them. They will know how to change not only their lives, but the lives of those around them. It is of supreme importance that people are grounded in the Word of God and do not rely solely upon an emotional experience. People must know that this new relationship with

God is not an emotional experience for a moment, but a decision that will change their lives now and for eternity. An emotional experience will not last nor will it make a lasting impact on their lives. When someone bases what they do on the Word of God, that Word will grow up and produce lasting fruit in their life. Remember, God says that His Word will not return void (Isaiah 55:11).

Your Example

As an effective witness, your example to a new Christian is very important. It is clear in the Bible that God sets high standards for the members of His family. Think about the importance of leading another person to salvation and the baptism of the Holy Spirit; the importance of altering the course of one's eternal destiny. This job requires your utmost authenticity. This means living a holy life every day.

"I beseech you therefore, brethren, by the mercies of God, that you present your bodies a living sacrifice, holy, acceptable to God, which is your reasonable service." Romans 12:1

As a representative of Jesus you need to set an example for those you minister to. You must be a man or woman of God who is committed to live a holy life. There are many Christians who smoke, drink, and are involved in negative behavior. Those things do not glorify God, nor are they an example of a holy lifestyle. You might wonder why some people struggle with these problems in their lives.

The Bible teaches us that until we get our minds renewed to the Word of God, we will not walk in God's perfect will, but will fight against the negative works of the flesh, which are listed in Galatians 5:19-21: "Now the works of the flesh are evident, which are: adultery, fornication, uncleanness, lewdness, idolatry, sorcery, hatred, contentions, jealousies, outbursts of wrath, selfish ambitions, dissensions, heresies, envy, murders, drunkenness, revelries, and the like; of which I tell you beforehand, just as I also told you in time past, that those who practice such things will not inherit the kingdom of God."

In addition to what God says about holiness, we also know we are His ambassadors and carry His name wherever we go. Let's say you just finished ministering to someone and they got born again. You have now become their example and image of what a Christian looks like. You have become a person of influence in that person's life. It is very natural that they would look to you as their example. They might ask you if they can still smoke or drink and how are you to answer them if your lifestyle is not in accordance with the Word of God? You cannot if you are still involved in the sin and negativity they need to be led out of.

As an example to others, you need to judge whatever you do in your life with a high level of seriousness. How would you feel if every Christian was behaving exactly as you are? If the answer to that question worries you then why do you do it? You do not have the right to do something you would tell a new Christian not to do. The Apostle Paul exhorted believers to follow him as he followed Christ. Someone should be able to watch you and do everything you do every day, and you would lead them right into the kingdom of God. You would be living a holy and upright life, and they would be as well. Continuously judge your life like that. James 1:22 says "But be doers of the word and not hearers only, deceiving yourselves". As we hear the Word and study the Word of God, we must learn to make our actions be in alignment with what the Bible teaches us.

"But as He who called you is holy, you also be holy in all your conduct, because it is written, 'Be holy, for I am holy.'" I Peter 1:15-16

The word 'conduct' in this passage means lifestyle. You must be holy in everything you say, think, and how you act. The goal is not to live under a rigid and strict law, but to live in His grace following a holy lifestyle. The Bible tells us to be holy in how we think, but you might be wondering why it matters. Although no one knows what you are thinking, God instructs us to have holy thoughts because He knows that whatever we think will come out in our words and actions; "For out of the abundance of the heart the mouth speaks," Matthew 12:34b.

As a leader to new Christians, you not only tell them how to live but you show them by example. More than likely, they will become the kind of Christian that you are. The most important things they learn will be caught, not taught; both consciously and unconsciously. They will follow you as they are in a completely new setting and you are their example. If you go to church, they will too. If you sit near the front of the church instead of the back, they will too. If you carry your Bible to church, they will too. If they see you lift your hands in praise and worship, they will too. If they observe you tithing and listening to the pastor, they will no doubt follow your example. In these and scores of other ways, you influence the entire course of their Christian life.

We must continue to encourage, guide, and build up these new Christians so they will grow up in the things of God and be strong in the Word. Remember how important you are to this new babe in Christ, and put aside anything that would hinder your example as you give yourself to minister.

Fear: Satan's Deception

The greatest tool the devil uses against the Christian is fear. Fear keeps us from loving people and helping them to be born again and filled with the Holy Spirit. Don't even entertain the thought of fear. Be confident in who you are in Christ and know that you are an able minister, and that God has called you to minister to people. If He has called you, know that He has enabled and equipped you to do it. I am going to warn you in advance: the devil will try to put fear in your mind in this area. You need to recognize where those thoughts come from. Cast down those imaginations and take those thoughts into captivity, (II Corinthians 10:5).

You may think, "What if I don't know what to say?" or "What if I misquote the scriptures?" The thoughts of fear and doubt are endless. Determine now that you are willing to face your fears and give yourself to the things of God and minister to others regardless of how you feel. Refuse to be focused on yourself and your own problems. The devil will try to convince you not to become trained and efficient in your knowledge of spreading the gospel of Jesus Christ. Don't allow him to bring that fear into your life. As you obey God and love people, that perfect love will cast out all fear. Your desire to help others will become bigger than your desire to succumb to your fears.

In His Word, God has commanded us to bring people into the Kingdom. He has told us that it is He who is working in us, and we are not on our own. When the devil tries to hinder you through fear, be wise and overcome his deception. Don't allow him to convince you of fear. Cast down those imaginations and take those thoughts into captivity. You have not been given the spirit of fear, but of power, and of love and of a sound mind. He has made you an able minister of the New Testament, and He is your sufficiency (II Corinthians 10:5, II Timothy 1:7, II Corinthians 3:5-6).

There are many ways the devil tries to attack us through fear. Don't listen to your physical symptoms, or your physical responses to fear. You might be shaking in your boots, you might be stumbling over your words, your mouth might be dry as cotton but these things are only physical responses to fear. There are many ways you might experience fear, but rise above those physical challenges and refuse to allow those things to stop you. Acknowledge that helping others know the saving love of Jesus Christ reigns supreme to your fears. If you step out in faith, and in obedience to what God has told you to do, you will be victorious. When you act in love, fear cannot remain (I John 4:18).

Feelings will deceive you; don't act according to your emotions or feelings. Come against that fear, and don't allow anything to stop you when sharing the gospel. You can do what the Word of God has commissioned you to do. You are an able minister!

3
Are You Qualified?

You Must be Born Again

The first requirement to being an effective witness is that you must be born again. You have to know that Jesus is your Savior. If you aren't confident in your salvation, how are you ever going to talk to someone else about it?

"That if you confess with your mouth the Lord Jesus and believe in your heart that God has raised Him from the dead, you will be saved. For with the heart one believes unto righteousness, and with the mouth confession is made unto salvation." Romans 10:9-10

You need to ask Jesus to be the Lord of your life, and believe that He died and was raised from the dead for you. By doing so, you commit your life to Him, and accept all that He has provided for you.

"Therefore, if anyone is in Christ, he is a new creation; old things have passed away; behold, all things have become new. Now all things are of God, who has reconciled us to Himself through Jesus Christ, and has given us the ministry of reconciliation." II Corinthians 5:17-18

As a new creature in Christ, we are given the

responsibility to spread the message. God has called us to bring all people into the kingdom of God. That is what the ministry of reconciliation is: helping other people to be born again. When you are in Christ, He makes you an able minister. He makes you able to tell others about Jesus.

You Must be Filled with the Holy Spirit

Being born again gets you into the kingdom of God, but being filled with the Holy Spirit enables you to be a success here on earth. To be a powerful witness for God on this earth you need to be filled with the Holy Spirit and regularly praying in other tongues.

> *"But you shall receive power when the Holy Spirit has come upon you; and you shall be witnesses to Me in Jerusalem, and in all Judea and Samaria, and to the end of the earth."*
> *Acts 1:8*

You need to know without a shadow of a doubt that you have the power and that it is working in you. I Corinthians 14:14-15 says: "For if I pray in a tongue, my spirit prays, but my understanding is unfruitful. What is the conclusion then? I will pray with the spirit, and I will also pray with the understanding. I will sing with the spirit, and I will also sing with the understanding." As a laborer in His harvest, you are ministering to other people. You are witnessing. With these tasks you need all God has provided for you to be able to do the works of the ministry. You need the strength and power that only the Holy Spirit can give you.

Praying in tongues on a regular basis releases that power and enables you to be an effective witness (praying in tongues, speaking in tongues, praying in the Holy Ghost, and praying in the Spirit, all mean the same thing.) In addition to interceding for the lost and praying them into the kingdom of God, you edify or strengthen your inner man when you pray in tongues, (I Corinthians 14:4). Then, you are ready to release power out of your innermost being.

"He who believes in Me, as the Scripture has said, out of his heart will flow rivers of living water. But this He spoke concerning the Spirit, whom those believing in Him would receive; for the Holy Spirit was not yet given, because Jesus was not yet glorified." John 7:38-39

Praying in the Holy Ghost has many benefits which will enable you to be a bold and effective witness. Study these benefits to know what they can do for you. Then you will be certain to pray in tongues regularly, and you will have the benefits manifested in your life. Listed below are seven benefits of praying in tongues.

1. Build up the inner man. I Corinthians 14:4 "He who speaks in a tongue edifies himself."

2. Intercede for the unknown. Romans 8:26

"Likewise the Spirit also helps in our weaknesses. For we do not know what we should pray for as we ought, but the Spirit Himself makes intercession for us with groanings which cannot be uttered."

3. Pray the perfect will of God. Romans 8:27 "Now He who searches the hearts knows what the mind of the Spirit is, because He makes intercession for the saints according to the will of God."

4. Builds you up on your faith. Jude 20 "But you, beloved, building yourselves up on your most holy faith, praying in the Holy Spirit."

5. Brings rest and refreshing. Isaiah 28:11-12 "For with stammering lips and another tongue He will speak to this people, to whom He said, 'This is the rest with which you may cause the weary to rest,' and, 'This is the refreshing'; yet they would not hear."

6. Gives thanks and magnifies God. Acts 10:46a "For they heard them speak with tongues and magnify God."

7. Tongues are a sign to unbelievers. I Corinthians 14:22a "Therefore tongues are for a sign, not to those who believe but to unbelievers."

A Leader of People

When you decide to be an effective witness, you are also deciding to be a leader. You are deciding to be the one who sets the example for those around you. As you minister to people, they will do the things you do, and they will say the things you say.

An effective witness is someone who has made the decision to stand up and be a leader in the body of Christ. There are many people who come to church all the time, but they have never made a decision to be a leader. If you want to reach people and change their lives forever, you must take on the responsibility of being a leader through example.

Qualifications of a Leader

There are some specific attitudes and behaviors that leaders have. As you train yourself to minister to others, there are some attitudes and behaviors you should develop. These are:

A leader believes in themselves. The Bible does not tell us to think lowly of ourselves. The Bible tells us to be confident and strong in who we are as Christians. Jesus says, in Matthew 28:20 "...Lo, I am with you always, even to the end of the age." He is telling us, "I live with you. I am with you" How dare we call ourselves anything less than what God calls us! How often do we call ourselves dumb, stupid, ugly, not worthy, not able, fearful, or unbelieving? How dare we say that about ourselves, when we have God living within us!

Almighty God Himself lives within us, and yet we talk negatively about ourselves. God says we are strong, creative, equipped, and able. We need to believe in ourselves the way God believes in us. God says in II Corinthians 3:5-6 that He has made us an able minister of the New Testament.

"But let each one examine his own work, and then he will have rejoicing in himself alone, and not in another." Galatians 6:4

God's way of thinking is not the same as the world's way. We need to renew our minds from the world's way to God's way. The world's way is to think badly of ourselves, and we are all trained in the world's way. If you go any place in the world, regardless of what continent or country it is, the devil has trained us to think lowly of ourselves.

Even extremely successful people who have made millions of dollars often don't believe in themselves the way God wants us all to. If you could get inside their hearts and minds, most of them have very low self-image and self-confidence. Celebrity figures are not excluded. In the natural, they have every material thing they could ever want, and yet they are often miserable. They may believe in their physical appearance, or their talent, but they really don't believe in themselves.

As a Christian, God lives inside of us! We are equipped with the best gift of all. One of the meanings of God's name is "Emmanuel." That literally means, "God in us, revealed in us." You can believe in yourself because you do not have to do anything alone, God lives in you. Through His equipping and empowering, you are able to do the work of the ministry.

"Not that we are sufficient of ourselves to think of anything as being from ourselves, but our sufficiency is from God, who also made us sufficient as ministers of the new covenant, not of the letter but of the Spirit; for the letter kills, but the Spirit gives life."
II Corinthians 3:5-6

This is a scripture that you should have underlined in your Bible, and have committed to your memory. I want you to especially note verse 6. This is the Holy Spirit directly speaking to you: "...who also made us sufficient as ministers of the new covenant..." God has made you an able minister of the New Testament!

An effective witness is a person who has committed themselves to be a leader. They recognize the calling of God on their life, and believe in themselves the way the Bible teaches them to. You are not supposed to think of yourself as nothing. You are not to think of yourself in a poor state of being. You must think of yourself the way God thinks and talks about you.

The Word says, "You are an able minister." As an able minister, you can boldly, and without any hesitation, minister to a person and get them born again and filled with the Holy Spirit. You can get them born again just by being a light, but when you are backed with the Word of God and the knowledge of exactly how to do it, you have an incredible strength supporting you. II Corinthians 5:17-18 says: **_"Therefore, if anyone is in Christ, he is a new creation; old things have passed away; behold, all things have become new. Now all things are of God, who has reconciled us to Himself through Jesus Christ, and has given us the ministry of reconciliation."_**

God has given to us the ministry of reconciliation or the task of resolving the gap between the lost and Christ. God has called us into the world to preach the gospel and reconcile the world unto Jesus Christ. Notice that we have been reconciled to Him, so now, we are to go out and reconcile others. We are to minister and we are to bring people into the kingdom of God. Verse 19 says: "... God was in Christ reconciling the world to Himself, not imputing their trespasses to them, and has committed to us the word of reconciliation." We have the ministry (calling) and we have the Word, what else could we need?

A leader is an ambassador. Many years ago while we were in the Philippines at a convention, Sir Lionel Luckoo opened the meeting. He was an ambassador for Uganda and had a very interesting job. Sir Lionel talked about himself as being an ambassador, as one who goes with authority and represents his own country in various countries. He knows full well the authority his country has given him, and he exercises that authority.

What about the spiritual calling we have as ambassadors for Christ? We are to go and do the work of the ministry. We are to represent our kingdom and our God with all power and authority, knowing the calling we have on our lives. II Corinthians 5:20 says: "Now then, we are ambassadors for Christ, as though God were pleading through us: we implore you on Christ's behalf, be reconciled to God." As God's ambassadors, you carry the authority to speak God's Word. Let it come out of your mouth boldly, with power, and authority, knowing that God has given you that right.

Remember that we did not earn either salvation or the right to be filled with the Holy Spirit. We did not receive it based on our merit. God gave it to us as a free gift. We are saved because God gave us our salvation; not because we have earned anything. Do not think that there is anything you can do to make God love you more or less. If you have failed to do everything perfectly; saying, "I didn't pray enough before I went to minister" or "I haven't studied the Bible as much as I should have," doesn't mean you should cease to witness to others. You cannot "earn" the opportunity to minister. Yes, you need to pray. Yes, you need to study the Bible. Yes, you need to strive to do the right things as an example, but you must do it because of the love in your heart and because you desire to be prepared.

God has given you the ministry of reconciliation, and He has said that He is your sufficiency. He has made you an able minister and an ambassador for Him. He does not give you the title as His ambassador one day, and revoke the title the next. God has called you as His ambassador, which is a statement of faith that He trusts you will be His voice and His example to those who need to see Him. Now, you are given the choice of what you will do with the title.

A leader is a giver. Leaders do not think of themselves first, they think of others and act selflessly towards people. Matthew 10:39 says: ***"He who finds his life will lose it, and he who loses his life for My sake will find it."***

When you are selfish and focus your attention on your needs and your desires, you cheapen your life mission. You lose the best that God has for you due to greed and self-centeredness. When you lose yourself and focus on the needs of others above your own, you will find your life. It may seem like a contradiction, but when we lose our lives for the sake of the gospel, we are rewarded immeasurably. Being a giver is an attitude and a way of life, not a one time decision or action. Givers don't obsess about what they give and keep track of everything. They freely plant seed and their harvest is plenty. A giver is always looking for a need to fill and a creative way in which they can fill it. Those who often find that they are short on time or resources are probably selfish with what they do have. The Bible very clearly teaches in Luke 6:38, as you start to sow seed, you will begin to reap a harvest, when you give it is given back to you.

A leader is committed. How committed you are to helping people will determine how effective you are. If you are committed and will do whatever it takes to see the harvest, you are ready to minster at any time. Being committed means being prepared when you are needed. You are committed to knowing the scriptures, and speaking up when the time is right.

If you are committed, you care enough to spend time in prayer interceding for the lost and building yourself up in the Spirit. You will be able to hear the leading of the Holy Spirit and minister correctly in any situation. The body of Christ needs committed leaders today – those spiritually prepared, and ready to get the work done.

A leader walks in love. The devil will always try to derail you before you even begin. He will give you countless opportunities to fight with your spouse or be angry towards someone about something. If you yield to that way of thinking, you will block the inclinations of the Holy Spirit and will hinder your ability to hear Him. When you have strife in your life, you cut off the flow of the Holy Spirit. It is as if a knot is in a hose and the water supply cannot get through.

Regarding gossip and complaining, I would like to make this point: be very careful how you talk about your church around your children. You are either bringing them into the church as productive members of the body of Christ, or you are forcing them out of the church and into the world. You are training them up in the way they should go by the things you do and say. Children will always grow up to do what you do, not what you say. Whether or not they make a conscious effort to do so, your children will act the way they see you act.

A leader speaks positively. As a leader it is essential that we maintain a positive approach to life. Gossiping and complaining will never bring effective change or beneficial results. There is always something to complain about if you give yourself permission. A mature Christian knows that the battle is not with people, but in the spirit realm; and is aware that complaining and a negative confession hinders rather than helps the situation. Rather than gripe and murmur, mature Christians are quick to intercede and believe for God's best in every situation.

If you murmur to yourself or to others, you have cut off your ability to hear from the Holy Spirit. You have cut off the anointing that will help you minister to people as needs arise. You might not like certain things at your church or in your job, but as a leader you realize your authority to bring change and growth is through prayer and intercession. It is at that point alone that a leader is prepared and ready to bring suggestions or ideas to those in charge. It is essential to always start and finish with prayer, this way we keep our heart and mind focused on God and His will.

You ARE a leader

Think of yourself as a leader, which is the way God sees you. Put the thought in your mind that you are a man or woman of God who is a leader in this life. You are the redeeming factor in this whole earth and you can do something amazing for God. You must see yourself that way and believe in yourself the way God believes in you; then nothing will stop you. If you do not believe what God says about you, you will not be able to minster to others effectively. You'll find yourself intimidated by them or afraid of them for one reason or another. It may be their age, fashion sense, or any number of issues, but something about them will make you feel inadequate. You will focus on your inferiority rather than on what God says about you. As a result, you will not be able to effectively give them the Word of God about salvation or the Holy Spirit. You will not be able to be the minister that God has called you to be.

Cast down the insecurities and false imaginations that exalt themselves against the knowledge of Christ. Cast down the strongholds of what you think you are, and believe what God says you are. Step out on the strength of His Word, and He will see to it that His Word does not return to you void.

One time I was sitting next to a woman on an airplane who was about 85 years old. I asked her if she knew Jesus and she responded, "Oh I hope so." I stopped right there, I didn't ask another question the rest of the flight. After all, she is my senior, how could I tell her anything she didn't already know? That is what I thought, but I see now that it was merely a lie of the devil to keep me from being the effective minister of the gospel, the ambassador for Christ, that God says I am.

You have to recognize who you are in Jesus Christ. You are His ambassador, His voice. What you do for a living, how much money you have, what type of education you have, or anything else does not matter at all. As a Christian you are called of God, therefore, He needs you. He has given you the ministry of reconciliation and you have a high calling on your life. God is working through you. You are a leader.

4
The Power to Witness

Prayer is the single-most important element in being an effective witness. It is what builds our own spirits and equips us to engage in the lives of others. The reason some churches are so successful in bringing people to Christ and getting them filled with the Holy Spirit is because there are many people, behind the scenes, who are praying and believing for these things to come to fruition. The churches that are not seeking the Lord through prayer, in their private times, often do not see the results of people being born again and filled with the Holy Spirit in their churches.

The battle is fought in the spirit realm. Through intercessory prayer, we break down the strongholds that satan has established in people's lives. In the spirit realm, we intercede for the lost, we bind the devil who has blinded people to the truth, and we fight for the lives of people. Our intercession allows the Holy Spirit to minister to them, and the scales to be lifted from their eyes so they can see the truth of the gospel. Through our prayer people are able to receive all that God has for them.

Simply having the desire to be the ambassador

God has called you to be is not enough. He has also told you in His Word about the importance of prayer. There is no way for you to effectively minister under the anointing of the Holy Spirit without having built yourself up in prayer. The time spent spiritually recharging your battery is significant. But, whether it is in the morning, or right before you minister, does not matter. The importance is that you are charged up in the Holy Spirit so you can hear His voice and minister under His direction (Jude 20). You are a child of God, and you are to be led by the Spirit in all you do. This is especially true when you are ministering God's Word to someone else. Be dedicated to prayer. Be committed to prayer. Do not waver in your spiritual charge but pray in the Holy Spirit regularly, for an extended period of time. Then you will see the fruit God has called you to produce.

Effective Prayer

When you pray for the lost, before ministering to them, you should pray with your understanding, (praying in English or whatever your native tongue is). Through prayer, the Bible says we send laborers (Christians) across their path to be a light and witness to them. You can bind the demonic authority, and free the people from any evil influence that would keep them from receiving what God has for them. You can keep their eyes from being blinded to the truth of the gospel - all when you intercede for them in prayer. The Bible says we have the power to believe for every person that comes into our life to be saved and filled with the Holy Spirit, (Luke 10:2; Matthew 12:29; John 12:40).

Praying in the understanding is important; however, praying in tongues should consume the major portion of your prayer time. In the understanding, our minds can only know so much and therefore we can only effectively pray for a small percentage of that which needs intercession. You do not know all the situations or attacks of the enemy that need to be fought against through prayer.

"Likewise the Spirit also helps in our weaknesses. For we do not know what we should pray for as we ought, but the Spirit Himself makes intercession for us with groanings which cannot be uttered." Romans 8:26

This scripture says, "The Spirit helps our weaknesses." That word "help" in the Greek means 'takes hold together with, against' our weaknesses. Weaknesses in this text means our inabilities. You can pray and get answers by speaking the Word of God in faith and in the name of Jesus for the situation; but there are many situations where you will not know the words to say in order to pray. The Holy Spirit knows what to pray, and you will always be praying the perfect will of God when you pray in tongues (Romans 8:27). The power of the Holy Spirit is released through you, and the prayer bypasses your mind or human intellect and starts working in countless areas. Through these two methods of prayer, you get things done in the spirit realm; praying in the understanding according to the Word of God in the name of Jesus, and praying in Holy Spirit.

What a terrific tool prayer is! Praise God for His amazing gift. If you are going to be an effective witness, and if you are going to be committed to ministering to the lost and helping people to receive the Holy Spirit, you need to understand the importance of prayer. If you are going to have the success God wants you to have, prayer must be a major part of your life.

When you are praying you are:
1. Standing in the gap. In Ezekiel 22:30 God says, *"So I sought for a man among them who would make a wall, and stand in the gap before Me on behalf of the land, that I should not destroy it; but I found no one."* That scripture will not be found true in your church, town, or area of the country if you are involved

in intercessory prayer. You will be standing in the gap for many people. God won't have to look any farther than you.

As you pray, God will see and know you are the one standing in the gap. His desire is that all people come to Him and are born again and filled with the Holy Spirit. If you are faithful to pray and call in the lost, plus you are dedicated and prepared to minister to the people, you will see many come to receive that which you already have. God will bring them to you as you are faithful: faithful in prayer, faithful to study the Word; and faithful to love and minister to people.

The more people that pray and intercede, the sooner we will experience what God wants accomplished. The concept of Won By One™ is that everyone does their part. If everyone you lead to salvation understands the importance of prayer, and they pray, they will be praying for someone you are not praying for. The Holy Spirit always knows God's perfect will and when we pray in the Holy Spirit, we will all effectively reach different people. As we pray in the Holy Spirit, it is in the Spirit, not our mind, that we pray His perfect will.

2. Strengthening your spirit man. I Corinthians 14:4 and Jude 20 tell us that *we edify ourselves and build ourselves up on our most holy faith by praying in the Holy Spirit.* We are not only interceding for others, we are strengthening our spirit man, as well. We could say we are charging up our spiritual battery. As we build ourselves up, we begin to become more sensitive to the Holy Spirit and more attentive to His voice. When the time comes to minister, we will have a clear vision from the Holy Spirit on what we need to do. The person who intercedes for the lost and is fully built up in prayer finds himself going to the right person, and has the right words to say for that situation. How can this be? The Holy Spirit guided him. If you are sensitive to the Holy Spirit, you will have a successful ministry. You can accomplish all that God has for you to do if you will pray according to His Word. Without that partnership with the Holy Spirit, you are doing works out of your own knowledge and understanding. You cannot consistently and successfully minister to others as God desires if your spirit man is not empowered by the Holy Spirit.

3. Making a commitment. Making a shift in our busy daily schedule is never an easy task. In order to find success in your prayer life you must make a conscious decision to make time in your day for prayer. If you do not make this decision to pray, you will not do it and your days will pass right before your eyes without you ever stopping and making time to pray.

You must make a commitment to pray, and

be responsible to fulfill that commitment. I have a specific time that I pray Monday through Friday and on Saturday and Sunday I have another time, due to my schedule being different. As an effective minister of the gospel you cannot afford to "try and find time." You must make time and make a commitment – a commitment as solid as the one you made when you got saved. It has to be that strong so that you will do it continuously. Once you see the difference in your life, and the increase of effectiveness for the work of the ministry, you will not go without it. Step out in faith on God's Word. He says if you will pray in other tongues, you will be edified. You will build yourself up on your most holy faith, and the Holy Spirit will pray the perfect will of God through you. Prayer should play an integral role in our lives as it serves to build us up and help those around us. Be committed to this benefit of being a strong Christian.

4. Praying in the understanding. You may be extremely intimidated with the concept of praying for any length of time in the understanding. Many people have never prayed for longer than 5 minutes at a time. God does not give us specific direction on how long to pray, but the idea of praying for 30 - 45 minutes seems nearly impossible. The best place to become more comfortable praying in the understanding is at an intercessory prayer meeting in someone's home or at church where you can listen to people who know how to pray. You will learn how to pray just like you learned how to praise God: by being around others who are doing it and learning from them.

If you are going to be involved with prayer and intercession, you not only need to pray in tongues, but you also need to know how to pray effectively in the understanding. There are three important elements to successful prayer in the understanding and without them prayer is merely words strung together that sound religious, but are unproductive. The three ingredients are:

1) Faith

2) The Word of God

3) The Name of Jesus

Being able to pray with these three elements will launch your prayer life to a new height. All three must be present at the same time. We pray the Word of God, in the name of Jesus while using our faith. Being able to pray the Word of God is important. God tells us to pray that His will be done on earth as it is in heaven; God's Word is His will. There are some excellent tools available for intercessors so we can become better skilled in prayer.

We must know the Word of God in order to pray His perfect will. Books that list scriptures in a topical manner and show how to pray are a necessity for praying the Word properly. As you use these tools to establish God's Word inside of you, the Holy Spirit will bring it to your remembrance and enable you to pray His Word without the help of the book. Praying the prayers written out in the book is a good way to pray effectively. Quoting scripture directly is another great way to pray effectively. There is power in the Word of God, and praying that power works!

5. Giving yourself to prayer. I Timothy 2:1-4 says: *"Therefore I exhort first of all that supplications, prayers, intercessions, and giving of thanks be made for all men, for kings and all who are in authority, that we may lead a quiet and peaceable life in all godliness and reverence. For this is good and acceptable in the sight of God our Savior, who desires all men to be saved and to come to the knowledge of the truth."* Notice that, in verse one, God says that first of all supplications, prayers, intercessions and giving of thanks be made for all people. God is saying that prayer is very important and it should be done first. Many times we put priorities on other things and reserve prayer for times of crisis or when we have extra time, but the Word tells us that our first priority must be prayer.

God has also given us the ability to pray even though we don't always know what to pray for, or how to pray for it. God has commanded us to pray for people in authority, for rulers and political officials. Do I know exactly what to pray for? There is no way for us to know the exact happenings of our president, the schedule of our governor, or the agenda of our law enforcement officers however, we are to pray for them. Even though I do not know what is going on, the Spirit of God does and He knows what their needs are. I pray through the Spirit of God, in other tongues. I pray so I can successfully fulfill I Timothy 2:1-4 in making intercession for all people; and I can know that I am praying perfectly because Romans 8:26 says the Spirit also helps my infirmities (inabilities to produce results), even if I don't know what to pray for.

"Likewise the Spirit also helps in our weaknesses. For we do not know what we should pray for as we ought, but the Spirit Himself makes intercession for us with groanings which cannot be uttered. Now He who searches the hearts knows what the mind of the Spirit is, because He makes intercession for the saints according to the will of God. And we know that all things work together for good to those who love God, to those who are the called according to His purpose." **Romans 8:26-28**

The Spirit of God is given to us for prayer, so we can pray for things we do not know about, He is our helper in prayer. He prays through us and covers our weaknesses and shortcomings. There are many times when you will not know what to say and you should give yourself to praying in the Holy Spirit. You should have a dedicated time when you pray in tongues. Along with your allotted time, you should create a lifestyle of praying in tongues. Pray in tongues whenever you can and remember that He is your constant friend.

I pray constantly throughout my day to keep myself built up on my most holy faith (Jude 20). When you are praying in the Holy Spirit, you are also benefiting yourself, not just the people around you. I Corinthians 2:10 teaches us that the Spirit of God will reveal things to us. We need to be sensitive and listen to the Spirit in order to know more about who He is. We must give ourselves to the Holy Spirit through these actions. We need to make a decision to be involved with the Holy Spirit through prayer constantly.

5

Steps to Salvation and Baptism with the Holy Spirit

I want to give you some simple steps that will show you how to get someone born again and baptized with the Holy Spirit. I have also included scriptures that correlate with each point. With these simple instructions, any born again believer can lead another person to salvation and being filled with the Holy Spirit!

Salvation – Step by Step

First of all, let's take a look at the steps to salvation. The scriptures that I quote in these steps should be read to the person you are ministering to. The scriptures I only list references for can be referred to when talking to the person, but do not need to be read.

Step 1:
Every person must be born again to know God and have everlasting life. John 3:3 says: "Jesus answered and said to him, '"Most assuredly, I say to you, unless one is born again, he cannot see the kingdom of God.'" (John 3:16)

Step 2:
The reason why we must be born again is found in Romans 3:23: "For all have sinned and fall short of the glory of God."

Step 3:
Romans 6:23 says you cannot earn salvation. I recommend that you quote this scripture to them since certain religions teach that salvation is earned by the works you do.

   a.There is nothing you can do on your own

   b.Salvation is God's gift to us (Ephesians 2:8-9)

Step 4:
Being saved or born again is receiving Jesus as your Lord (Master), and committing yourself to follow His Word. Romans 10:9-10 says: "That if you confess with your mouth the Lord Jesus, and believe in your heart that God raised Him from the dead, you shall be saved. For with the heart one believes unto righteousness, and with the mouth confession is made unto salvation." (I John 2:3)

Step 5:
Ask the person: "Are you ready to make this life changing commitment; to change from your way to accept Jesus' way?

Step 6:
If they are ready, pray and lead the person into a confession of faith. Make sure they ask Jesus to be their Lord. Here is an example of a prayer you might lead them in: "God, I come to you in the name of Jesus and I ask you to come into my life. I confess that Jesus is my Lord, and I believe in my heart that You have raised Him from the dead. I turn my back on sin, renounce all other religions and commit to follow You for the rest of my life. I am now a child of God. Thank you, Father, for saving me!"

Step 7:
You are now born again, forgiven, and on your way to heaven, (II Corinthians 5:17). Yet, this is only the beginning. You need to renew your mind to live the victorious life God has provided for you. Romans 12:1-2 says: "I beseech you therefore, brethren, by

the mercies of God, that you present your bodies a living sacrifice, holy, acceptable to God, which is your reasonable service. And do not be conformed to this world, but be transformed by the renewing of your mind, that you may prove what is that good and acceptable and perfect will of God."

 a. You must grow and learn God's Word (Romans 10:17).

 b. You must be fed regularly (Hebrews 10:25).

Step 8:

If doubts or fears come to mind about your salvation, reject them and realize that the Bible is what your new birth is based on, and not what you think or feel (Romans 10:9-10).

Step 9:

You will need to be baptized in water as a believer (Mark 16:15-17).

Step 10:

God has also given us another gift, which is the baptism of the Holy Spirit. May I show you what the Bible teaches us...

From here you can go right into the steps to the baptism of the Holy Spirit. The transition from one to the other is very simple and easy. If they are not willing to go on at this point, you can stop by rejoicing with them. Show them how excited you are for them and what a good decision they have made. Make sure they know that they need to be baptized in water as a believer (Mark 16:15-17).

Baptism with the Holy Spirit - Step by Step
Step 1:
Have you confessed Jesus as Lord? (Romans 10:9-10)
Step 2:
Let's look at Who the Holy Spirit is:

a.John 14:26 says: "But the Helper, the Holy Spirit, whom the Father will send in My name, He will teach you all things, and bring to your remembrance all things that I said to you." He is your comforter and teacher. He helps you in everyday situations.

b.Acts 1:8 says: "But you shall receive power when the Holy Spirit has come upon you; and you shall be witnesses to Me in Jerusalem, and in all Judea and Samaria, and to the end of the earth." He is your power, abundant strength, and ability to be an overcomer, and live a victorious life.

Step 3:
What happens when you are filled? Acts 2:4 says: "And they were all filled with the Holy Spirit and began to speak with other tongues, as the Spirit gave them utterance." You will speak in tongues. This is the first evidence of being baptized with the Holy Spirit.

a. The Holy Spirit is already here for every born again person. You don't have to wait or work for Him.

b.Acts 2:38-39 refers to the Holy Spirit as being a gift to every believer.

Step 4:
Your mind will not understand or gain anything from tongues; it will sound useless and foolish to the natural mind. You are speaking mysteries to God, not to man. I Corinthians 14:2 says: "For he who speaks in a tongue does not speak to men but to God, for no one understands him; however, in the spirit he speaks mysteries." I Corinthians 14:14-15

says: "For if I pray in a tongue, my spirit prays, but my understanding is unfruitful. What is the conclusion then? I will pray with the spirit, and I will also pray with the understanding. I will sing with the spirit, and I will also sing with the understanding." Speaking in tongues is an act of your will. God will not force you to do it, or do it for you.

Step 5:
If you ask for the Holy Spirit in faith, you will receive. Luke 11:13 says: "If you then, being evil, know how to give good gifts to your children, how much more will your heavenly Father give the Holy Spirit to those who ask Him!"

Step 6:
Ask the person if they have any questions. If not, are they ready to receive the Holy Spirit?

Step 7:
Have the person ask for the Holy Spirit (Luke 11:13), then lead them into a confession of thanking God for filling them with the Holy Spirit. An example is: "Father, I come in the name of Jesus, and I thank you for filling me with Your Holy Spirit right now. I receive Him with the evidence of praying in other tongues. I will pray out boldly in other tongues right now in Jesus' name." After praying this prayer, both of you will begin to pray in tongues.

Step 8:
Praying in tongues regularly will build (edify) or charge up the spirit man. Jude 20 says: "But you, beloved, building yourselves up on your most holy faith, praying in the Holy Spirit."

Step 9:
They need to be baptized in water if they haven't yet as a believer (Acts 2:28; and Mark 16:15-17).

Ministering salvation

When you begin to talk with a person, and feel that they need Jesus, simply ask them if they are born again. It is very important that you do not assume anything relative to the person's background. You need to be certain that they either are or are not saved. Most likely, if the person is saved according to Romans 10:9-10, they will be able to tell you when they were born again, and how they did it. It is not good enough for them to say, "God has always been a part of my life," or "I've always known the man upstairs." You need to ask them specifically if they are born again or if they are saved (those mean the same thing). Ask key questions that will better enable you to minister to their particular needs.

Knowing a person's church background may enable you to answer questions you know they have, or clear up areas of question that have been keeping them from receiving all God has for them. They may think they are born again, or they may think they have always been a Christian, but unless they have made Jesus their Lord, and are committed to follow Jesus according to Romans 10:9-10, they are not born again.

For example, if you are ministering to someone who has come from a Catholic, Mormon, or Jehovah's Witness background, you will want to emphasize to them that salvation is a gift of

God, and not something we earn by the works we do. When you minister to someone from a "religious" background, you must be very clear about what the Word of God says. Religion will not save someone. Works will not save someone. Being involved with a cult will not save someone. Doing what the Word of God says will!

As an effective witness, you must be strongly established in God's Word, because many people believe that if you are a Catholic, or a Baptist, or a Methodist, etc., you are automatically going to heaven! That is not true. Many "religions" do not teach that you must be born again according to Romans 10:9-10. Some don't even acknowledge Jesus as the Son of God. Once you find out what kind of religious background a person has come from, you must be very clear about what the Word of God says about being born again and filled with the Holy Spirit. Make sure that you minister in love and not with the pompous attitude that you are right, and they are wrong.

I was raised in the Methodist church. My father was even a pastor, but I was not born again. I didn't know what the Bible said about being born again. I never read my Bible, and no one in the church ever told me about being born again. When you are sharing with someone, do not assume they know something just because they grew up in a certain church. Chances are, they don't know what the Bible says about being born again and filled with the Holy Spirit. They may know what their denomination says, or what someone else says, but all that matters is what the Word of God says.

Once you have determined a person's needs and some of their background, you can begin to go through the scriptures and minister to that person. You might start by saying, *"Every person must be born again to know God and to have everlasting life."* **Turn to John 3:3** and read it to them.

Then go right into, "The reason you must be born again is found in Romans 3:23: **"...for all have sinned and fall short of the glory of God"** These scriptures are in a very specific order because they are teaching a person step-by-step on why they are making the choice to accept Jesus.

Romans 6:23 is one of the scriptures that you would quote: **"For the wages of sin is death, but the gift of God is eternal life through Christ Jesus our Lord."** It is not necessary that you look this scripture up.

After you have quoted it explain that the way they are living is going to lead to death but Jesus has given us a free gift, which is life everlasting. Keep in mind that too many scriptures can confuse a person. It is a good idea to just quote some scriptures.

After you have explained that Jesus gives life everlasting, explain that they cannot earn salvation. Say, *"There is nothing you can do on your own. It is a gift of God, not something earned by working or trying to be good."*

"Being saved or born again, is receiving Jesus as your Lord and your Savior, and committing yourself to follow His Word, the Bible." Then you would read Romans 10:9-10. Once you have read that scripture, you might say, *"Do you believe that God raised Jesus from the dead?"* Once they say that they do believe, you can then ask if they are ready to make the life-changing commitment to make Jesus their Lord.

Some people don't like the word "commitment," but that is exactly what becoming a Christian is about, it is a life-changing commitment. Don't lighten that reality up at all. They must recognize it as a life-changing commitment and they have to choose between the god of this world and God the Father. They must accept Jesus as their only Savior and make Him their Lord. Make that very clear.

If you have just read Romans 10:9-10 to them, and don't explain what it means to make someone their Lord they can easily miss the point. They might think that all they have to do is say with their mouth that Jesus is their Lord, and that will get them saved. You might ask them, *"Do you know what it means to make someone your Lord?"* Before they can answer, go ahead and tell them that it means making them your boss, and whatever they say, you are sure to do. So, if Jesus is your Lord, He is your Boss. In order for you to do what He wants you to do, you have to do what the Bible says.

The Bible is the Word of God, and that's what Jesus wants you to follow. When you make Jesus your Lord, what you're doing is deciding to turn from your way of doing things, your old way of living, and your old way of thinking; and follow Jesus as your Lord and Savior. You must follow Him according to what the Bible says.

Once the person makes this decision you lead them in the confession of faith. Use a very simple prayer, such as, **"God, I come to you in the name of Jesus..."** (Don't open the prayer with "Father," because He is not their Father, as of yet. They are not born again.) **"...I ask you to come into my life, I confess that Jesus is Lord, and I believe in my heart that You have raised Him from the dead. I turn my back on sin and renounce all other religions. I am now a child of God. Thank you, Jesus!"**

This prayer is not for you to memorize word for word, it is a basic prayer that contains all the ingredients a person needs to be born again. Let me caution you about using a lot of frills. Don't be guilty of being repetitious. Stay clear of adding a lot of flowery, religious language as this way of communication will surely go right over the person's head. Be very clear and basic so that there are no questions. We want them to understand exactly what he/she is saying, and the exact result of these statements.

Don't eliminate the part about renouncing other religions. The Holy Spirit gave me that word very strongly when I was in the Philippines. He said, "Wendy, it is a necessity that you have people renounce anything that would hold them back." It came to me strongly in the Philippines because there is a lot of witchcraft, religion and a lot of things about Catholicism that are not practiced in the U.S. Even in America, people worship other things and these practices cannot continue once Jesus is their Lord. Go through it with confidence and clarity, and they will follow right along.

The prayer is one that, as you lead them, they will repeat after you. Do not give them too many words to remember, or too few words to speak either. Lead them with enough words each time so they can follow along and it still flows smoothly. Keep an entire thought together. Make it easy for them to understand exactly what they are saying.

Once you have finished the prayer, continue to follow the steps. Explain to them that they are now born again and on their way to heaven, yet that step was only the first step. Explain the importance of renewing your mind to live the victorious life God has for each one of us. Many people have been born again, and then they go and do their own thing. You must show the person the importance of studying God's Word and renewing their mind to what it says. Their thinking must come into alignment with God's thinking.

"I beseech you therefore, brethren, by the mercies of God, that you present your bodies a living sacrifice, holy, acceptable to God, which is your reasonable service. And do not be conformed to this world, but be transformed by the renewing of your mind, that you may prove what is that good and acceptable and perfect will of God." Romans 12:1-2

They must grow and be trained on the Word of God and be fed regularly. This is what you really want to implant in them. If they get born again in your church, they should come back to your church unless they live far away and are just visiting. Church is where they need to get their spiritual food on a continual basis. Let them know that they need to come back to church and be fed the Word of God in a community setting.

When babies are born into the world, they must be taught everything; how to walk, talk, and live. As a newborn Christian, we also must be taught how to walk and talk in the way that Jesus teaches us to live. Make them aware that they must get involved in a church under a pastor who teaches the Bible. They need to learn God's Word in a practical and relevant manner in order to become strong as a Christian. Also, explain to them that when doubt and fear enter their mind, they were born again based on the Word of God and it was a decision made by faith in accordance with what they read in Romans 10:9-10. It doesn't matter how they feel, what matters is God's promise to save them.

Water baptism is another step that they must take after they have become born again. Being baptized in water is simply done out of obedience to the Bible and is not an option for believers. Being baptized in water does not save us; it is an outward expression of what has already taken place spiritually.

Mark 16:16 says: ***"He who believes and is baptized will be saved; but he who does not believe will be condemned."*** Jesus made water baptism a very important step in your relationship with Him. Water baptism as a believer is not the same thing as being christened or sprinkled when you were a child. At that time, you weren't old enough to make the choice to believe in Jesus and therefore did not make the choice to be baptized.

The Bible says that once you believe, you must be baptized. You are baptized in water in obedience to the Word of God and as an outward expression of the unseen spiritual decision.

Remember when ministering to people to let the Bible speak for itself. The Bible is powerful and people are drawn to the saving power of Jesus. We do not need to defend or justify the contents. Be confident in the message of Christ. Put the Word out there and let it stand on its own.

After the person is saved, offer them the baptism of the Holy Spirit. Explain how God has given us another gift that equips and empowers us to live with comfort and clarity throughout our daily lives—the Holy Spirit. Show them what the Bible says about the Holy Spirit, if they are open to it, lead them into the scriptures. If they are not open to it then do not push the subject.

Baptism of the Holy Spirit

In helping someone receive the baptism of the Holy Spirit, they must first be born again. Never assume because someone has been around church or around Christians, they are born again. Simply because someone can use the common church terminology does not mean they are born again or filled with the Holy Spirit, and we are not to assume they are.

The Bible tells us the world cannot receive the

Holy Spirit. A person must first be born again and then filled with the Holy Spirit.

"The Spirit of truth, whom the world cannot receive, because it neither sees Him nor knows Him; but you know Him, for He dwells with you and will be in you." John 14:17

Ask them how they know they are born again; this is not to embarrass but to ensure that they truly have confessed and believe that Jesus is their Savior. If they respond by flippantly saying they have been born again since they were young, ask them when and where they were born again. Remember to respond in kindness and love, but the issue of salvation mustn't be carelessly overlooked. This is the most important decision they have ever made, or hopefully will make shortly.

You can usually tell when a person is truly born again, but if you have any questions at all, do not let it pass by unchallenged. It never hurts to go through the simple steps of salvation again; afterwards you both will have confidence in their eternity.

At this point, show them who the Holy Spirit is. Remember that the Holy Spirit is the third Person of the Godhead and is "He", not an "it". Turn together to John 14:26, and show them that

He is their Comforter and Teacher. He is the one who helps them in their every day life and is their power to live victoriously and to witness, as shown in Acts 1:8. You are showing them who the third person of the Trinity is, and that they can receive Him.

"And they were all filled with the Holy Spirit and began to speak with other tongues, as the Spirit gave them utterance." Acts 2:4

Next, show them what happens when you are filled with the Holy Spirit. Share with them that the Holy Spirit is available for every born again Christian, and that you don't have to work, or wait for Him. The evidence of being filled with the Holy Spirit is beginning to speak with other tongues. Every person who is filled with the Holy Spirit has the ability to pray in other tongues; the gift is given to all believers, not given to just an exclusive group. God is not a respecter of persons, He freely gives His gifts to ALL people (Acts 2:38-39).

"For he who speaks in a tongue does not speak to men but to God, for no one understands him; however, in the spirit he speaks mysteries." I Corinthians 14:2

With our human mind we do not understand

what it means to pray in tongues. Your natural mind will not know what you are saying. Explain to them that praying in tongues is an act of their will. I Corinthians 14:15 says: *"...I will pray with the spirit, and I will also pray with the understanding..."* Make it clear that you must chose to pray in the Holy Spirit. It is not going to happen without our blatant desire and obedience. Just as we have decided to talk to God through prayer in English or our native language; we also decide to pray in the Holy Spirit.

When we decide to take the step to pray in tongues, the Holy Spirit is our helper. Explain that although we must use our mouth and vocal chords, they are teaming with the Holy Spirit and working together. God will not do it for them, nor can they do it without God. As they open their heart up in obedience to Him, the Holy Spirit fills them and they work together as a team.

The Bible says, "...when you ask..." Make sure that they ask for the Holy Spirit, you cannot do it for them. Similar to the prayer of salvation, lead them in the prayer of receiving the Holy Spirit. Such as, ***"Father, I ask you to fill me with the Holy Spirit, with the evidence of praying in other tongues. I receive Him from You and according to the Bible, I will pray out boldly in other tongues right now, in Jesus' name."***

The guideline I have explained is just a

guideline, but remember to keep the scriptures in the order given, as to avoid confusion. Also, remember to explain what will happen after the two of you pray together. Tell them that once the prayer is concluded, you both are going to begin to pray out in other tongues.

Before you pray for them, tell them you will put your hand on their shoulder as a point of contact. I have never had anyone say no, but tell them first to avoid any shock or discomfort. Then have them pray, by leading them through the prayer.

As soon as you conclude the prayer, begin praying in tongues and they will also. A few hints: Have them close their eyes, but you keep yours open. If they have not opened their mouth, try to encourage them to speak out boldly, and continue to pray in tongues yourself. When you pray, pray boldly! The person you are praying with will match your volume; if you whisper and are bashful, they will follow suit.

Be bold and confident in your gift of praying in the Holy Spirit. If they still do not respond, stop and ask them gently what is going on with them. Find out if they have questions, are still nervous, or don't know what to do; but don't be afraid to ask what is going on. Always go back to the scripture to help them overcome what is hindering them. You may want to show them I Corinthians 14:15 again, and tell them it is an act of their will.

And that they need to speak out. God won't force them or do it for them. Then, go ahead and pray in tongues with them.

Never refer to the first words someone speaks, when they are filled with the Holy Spirit, as "baby talk". Initially, a person may not have a large vocabulary, but they are not talking "baby talk". I have heard many people use this analogy that the first words you speak in tongues are similar to that of a baby's first words. Then, as you grow older, you have a more developed language. The Bible says we receive a language. Yes, we do need to grow in our language so that it becomes fluent, but we start speaking a language.

If you were to go to school to learn a different language, you wouldn't start off by using baby babblings, you would start off by learning actual words that mean something. You don't immediately know the whole dialect, but you learn words. When you receive your prayer language, you receive words of a language from God. You are being filled with the power of God, and you receive a language, a very specific and unique prayer language between you and God. It is a language for you to pray specifically to God to intercede for yourself and the world.

Once you have prayed with someone to be born again or filled with the Holy Spirit, let them tell you what happened, or what they have received. Don't tell them that they have got it, ask them to explain to you what they have, or what they were doing. Let them speak it out of their own mouth, because they will believe what they say. If you tell them, they could question it, doubt it, and wonder whether it was real or not; but if they tell you what happened to them, they will not lie about it.

There have been some instances where people have tried to fool the person praying with them. They would pretend to speak in tongues, but when they were asked what they were doing, they honestly said that they were just making up some words. Now, if the person praying with them had exclaimed that they had gotten it, and not further questioned them, they would have left and not received.

Once the person tells you what they received, pray with them again in tongues. This time, make sure you don't touch them, so that they know that they can do it on their own. After you are done praying the second time, ask them again what they received. Once they tell you again, you can be excited with them and say that you are their witness. Verbally reinforce that you heard and saw them pray in other tongues! This excitement and declaration strengthens their decision within them.

It is important to always have the person pray

in tongues more than one time. They need to know for sure what has happened, and that it is not a one-time, special event. They need to know that, when they leave you, they can pray in tongues whenever and wherever they want to. They need to know they control it, and it is not something that controls them (I Corinthians 14:15).

Now that they have prayed and are confident with it, share with them Jude 20. Show them that the Bible says praying in tongues builds them up. It charges them up and gets them in touch with the power they have received, the Holy Spirit. Tell them to pray in tongues at least five minutes a day to start. Let them know it is important to pray every day, to stay built up, as Jude 20 says. The decision to accept the Holy Spirit and accept the language He gives is one of the best decisions we could ever make.

6

Helpful Hints and Common Questions

Study to Show Yourself Approved

I cannot emphasize this point enough. To effectively minister salvation and the baptism of the Holy Spirit to someone, you must have the scriptures on the inside of you. When you know the scriptures, as well as the order they go in, you can minister with confidence. There is a great difference between being familiar with the passages, and having them memorized so that you truly know them. When you are only familiar with the passages, there is always the possibility of forgetting them when you really need it, or when you get nervous; but if you know something in your spirit, the Holy Spirit can bring it to your remembrance when you are ministering to someone.

Occasionally, when you are ministering to someone, you'll find it necessary to use the person's Bible to whom you are ministering. People tend to have a lot more confidence in what you are saying when you can use their Bible and move confidently through it. They know it's true because you used their Bible and were sure about what you were saying and reading.

Practice the scriptures and the steps. You should practice them so much that, when you are actually ministering to someone, you are able to concentrate on the person and their reaction to what you are saying. It is important to be attentive to their needs, rather than concerned with the steps, and scriptures that you are proceeding through. If you can concentrate on the person rather than what you have to say next, the Holy Spirit can work through you much more effectively and powerfully. Ask your friends and family members to let you "practice" on them. Who knows, they might get saved themselves!

When you know the scriptures, Satan will not be able to come against you with fear tactics. He won't be able to make you uptight about ministering to someone. You will be confident and fully assured that the Holy Spirit will work through you, because you know the scriptures in your spirit, not just in your head.

Your Appearance
"We give no offense in anything, that our ministry may not be blamed." II Corinthians 6:3

We do not want anything about us, including our appearance, to distract the person we are trying to minister to. It is important that we create an avenue for the person to be open to receive from God; this includes being professional in our appearance and conduct. I am not talking about spending a lot of money on designer clothing in order to look a certain way. In order to be effective you need to be clean and neat, which includes smelling good. Think about the practical things: Do I need a breath mint? Did I put on too much cologne or forget my deodorant? We want to try to maximize Jesus and minimize ourselves as we set out to minister His Word.

Stay on Track

When you are ministering to someone to get them born again and/or filled with the Holy Spirit, it is good to remember that you are not there to counsel them. You are there to help them with their eternal destiny. If they start to ask you for guidance and counsel on other issues, advise them that you are not a licensed counselor. You can pray for them, be kind, and if they do need counseling, make sure they know that is not your role.

Watch Your Words!

When you are helping someone to be born again or filled with the Holy Spirit, don't speak "christianese". Christian lingo can be very confusing to a new Christian. Avoid using phrases like "the Word says", as they don't even know what "the Word" is. They are most likely not going to understand words like redemption, repentance, sanctification, or carnally minded. These are all words that are found throughout the Bible, and until they become familiar with it, they will not understand their meanings. Be simple in phrasing biblical concepts. They know who Jesus is, I recommend saying *"Jesus says..."* In Matthew 13:19, Jesus says, *"When anyone hears the word of the kingdom, and does not understand it, then the wicked one comes and snatches away what was sown in his heart. This is he who received seed by the wayside."*

When you are sowing the Word of God, you have to make sure people understand it. If they do not, satan will try to come in and steal the Word from them. Make sure they understand each point before you go on to the next one. Be specific and don't be afraid to ask them if they have any questions or need something clarified. The devil earnestly desires to spread confusion; he does so by sowing seeds of uncertainty so the words you are ministering to the person cannot produce fruit. Speak clearly and with terminology they understand, then there will be no confusion and God's Word is clearly understood.

You Set the Tone

When you are praying with someone, be sure that you don't talk too loudly or too quietly. Talk in a normal tone that lets your confidence come through yet still creates a peaceful and comfortable environment. Be sure to speak clearly so they understand what you are saying but use a natural, medium-range voice level. As you speak, be attentive to them to ensure they fully understand all you say. Remember that they will follow you, so be natural in your vocal levels as you pray.

What Bible translation should I use?

Any direct translation of the Bible is fine: King James Version, New King James Version, New International Version, etc.

There are some translations that are not the best to use when ministering. Remember that clarity and understanding is very important when ministering the Word. Paraphrased versions like, *The Message Bible,* are generally not good to use. A paraphrased version is one where someone reads the scriptures, and then writes what they think it says. It is not translated from the original Greek and Hebrew texts, but instead the ideas are expressed in a way that we would talk now, in modern language. It is certain that a doctrinal belief is going to come through when someone writes their personal "interpretation" of what the scripture says. These versions can be great for personal devotion and growth, but not recommended when working with someone for salvation or receiving the Holy Spirit.

Stay with the standard translations, and you will avoid trouble with clarity and interpretation. You will also be helping them become solid and established on a translation to study and grow from. If you don't know what kind to purchase, you can ask a Christian bookstore for their recommendation.

Can I help more than one person at a time?

There are times when you may need to minister to a whole group at once. This situation is a very simple one to work with, although it is not necessarily ideal. Proceed through the steps noted in Chapter 5 and read them the appropriate scriptures. At this point ask if anyone has a question. If someone is confused on a simple issue, address the question by reaffirming them with the scripture. If they say they are unsure if this is right for them, kindly tell them that you will talk specifically with them in a moment. Do not get involved in a deep conversation right then, and avoid debates or arguments completely. One person's negativity will negatively affect the rest of the group.

After you have answered any questions they have, lead them collectively into a confession of faith. At this point flow right into the steps explaining the baptism of the Holy Spirit. After you have led them through the prayer of receiving the Holy Spirit, begin to pray in tongues and encourage them to pray as well. Lay your hands on their shoulders (remember to inform them of what you are doing) and continue to pray out with boldness. If you are by yourself and are praying for many people, you cannot lay your hands on them all. Tell them that after you pray, you will say, "Now be filled, and begin to speak in other tongues." At this point they should all be praying in other tongues. Encourage them that it is an act of their will and takes boldness, even though you are in a group.

This will work exactly the same way with one person, a group of people, or thousands of people. The Word of God is true and is effective for any number of people. Be bold and confident because you know what the Word of God has to say. If some are not receiving, finish with the main group and then help the others individually.

What if someone wants to argue?

If a person has an argumentative attitude, it is very hard to give them any form of instruction. You cannot teach someone who is unwilling to receive; you will only receive a blot in return. If you start to minister to someone who wants to argue, you should end the conversation as quickly as possible. II Timothy 2:23-24 says: ***"But avoid foolish and ignorant disputes, knowing that they generate strife. And a servant of the Lord must not quarrel but be gentle to all, able to teach, patient."***

Try to avoid asking foolish questions such as, *"Do you believe in the Bible?"* This could invoke a negative response from the person you are ministering to, as they may answer, "no."

If you are ministering to someone who is consumed with persuading you to believe what they are saying, kindly end the conversation and believe the seeds you planted took root in their heart.

What about confessing all my sin?

It is common for people to try to confess their sins before receiving salvation. I John 1:9 says: ***"If we confess our sins, He is faithful and just to forgive us our sins and to cleanse us from all unrighteousness."*** Many people misuse this scripture when ministering the gospel of salvation to others. It is important to reference verse 6 before making assumptions about verse 9. I John 1:6 says: ***"If we say that we have fellowship with Him, and walk in darkness,*** *we lie and do not practice the truth."*

This verse is referring to believers and says, *"If we say we have fellowship with Him..."* This is not referring to an individual who has not dedicated their life to Christ. It says in verses 7-9: **"But if we walk in the light, as He is in the light, we have fellowship with one another, and the blood of Jesus Christ, His Son, cleanses us from all sin. If we say that we have no sin, we deceive ourselves, and the truth is not in us. If we confess our sins, He is faithful and just to forgive us our sins and cleanse us from all unrighteousness."**

These scriptures are clearly speaking to a person who is "in the light" and who is already a Christian. A person who has not been born again is not walking in the light, but in darkness, and therefore not held to the standard Christians are held to.

In order to be born again, one must confess with their mouth that Jesus is Lord, and believe in their heart that God raised Him from the dead. They do not have to confess their sins, as their entire life prior to being saved has been sinful. Once we have made the choice to be born again, we then confess our sins to God, and He cleanses us from all unrighteousness.

We know that God will always forgive us of our sins when we confess them to Him. This does not mean we are allotted safe passage to live in sin and confess when we deem it necessary to be done with our sinful ways. As a born again believer, we are called to live at higher standard and to live holy on this earth.

The belief that one must confess all of their sins before they can be born again is based out of the idea that one must earn God's love; or work your way into heaven by taking the proper steps. There is nothing that we can do to earn God's love, it is a gift that He freely gives to us, and is given purely by His love for us. It is through God's grace that we are saved and filled with the Holy Spirit. Ephesians 2:8-9 says: ***"For by grace you have been saved through faith and that not of yourselves; it is the gift of God, not of works, lest anyone should boast."***

If I get saved – do I have to quit....?

As pastors, we often hear questions filled with people's concern about what they can and can't do now that they are saved. New Christians always want to know, now that they are saved do they have to stop smoking, or drinking, or living with their girlfriend. We never answer their questions with a long list of scriptures. The best way to answer their question is by asking them the same question, and let them answer it themselves. *"Do you think you should be drinking?"* Often times they already know the answer, which is why they asked it in the first place. Most of the time, they will answer that they know they should not be participating in that sin.

When you are ministering to someone to be born again, remember that they are just stepping out of the world's way of living, and are making a dramatic shift in their lifestyle. There are many things that are normal behavior for people who are living in the world, which we no longer participate in; be gracious and patient when showing them what the Word has to say about worldly behavior.

I thought I got the Holy Spirit when I got saved...

Many churches teach that when you are born again, you also receive the Holy Spirit, and you receive all that there is to receive. It is true that, when they were born again, they were born of the Spirit (John 3:16, Galatians 4:29), but they were not filled with the Spirit. The baptism of the Holy Spirit is a separate act that follows salvation.

It is very important that when communicating this to a new believer that you are careful to show them exactly what the Word says, as this is a very delicate topic. Satan has built up this area of confusion amongst many denominations and caused resentment between believers based on different beliefs of the Holy Spirit. When you are ministering, go directly to the Bible and show them what it says about the Holy Spirit.

"He said to them, 'Did you receive the Holy Spirit when you believed?' So they said to him, 'We have not so much as heard whether there is a Holy Spirit.' And he said to them, 'Into what then were you baptized?' So they said, 'Into John's baptism.' Then Paul said, 'John indeed baptized with a baptism of repentance, saying to the people that they should believe on Him who would come after him, that is, on Christ Jesus.' When they heard this, they were baptized in the name of the Lord Jesus. And when Paul had laid his hands on them, the Holy Spirit came upon them, and they spoke with tongues and prophesied." Acts 19:2-6

We see in this passage that Paul clearly distinguished the two acts as being separate events during a person's Christian life. The people Paul was preaching to were already saved and baptized in the name of Jesus, but had not been filled with the Holy Spirit. After he confirmed that all had received salvation, he laid his hands on them and the Holy Spirit came upon them, with the evidence of speaking in other tongues.

We see throughout the New Testament many instances where people were saved in the name of Jesus, but had not yet been filled with the Holy Spirit. In Acts 8:12, 14-17 we see Peter and John going to Samaria and praying for the believers, both men and women, and when they laid their hands upon them every one was filled with the Holy Spirit, and began to pray in other tongues.

The Holy Spirit is a gift that is given to us by our Heavenly Father. Luke 11:13 says: *"If you then, being evil, know how to give good gifts to your children, how much more will your heavenly Father give the Holy Spirit to those who ask Him!"* Jesus is telling His disciples that, if they ask, their Heavenly Father would give them the Holy Spirit. We know that they must have already been saved in order to call God their Heavenly Father.

Once you have shown these scriptures to the person you are ministering to, they will easily see that the baptism of the Holy Spirit is separate from being born again.

What if they don't pray in tongues immediately?

Don't panic! It is okay if you lay your hands on someone to be filled with the Holy Spirit, and they don't immediately start praying in tongues. There are many reasons why someone might not begin to pray in tongues immediately. Often times, people are nervous and scared to begin praying in a new language. Your confidence is essential at this point, encourage them and be patient with them as they begin to speak out. Remember that you are there to help them start something new; if they begin to move their lips, encourage them to continue praying out loud.

Some people may not pray out at all, and a very few may not even try. The Holy Spirit will never force His presence, but is always there when we open up to Him. If the person you are ministering to does not open their mouth to speak, remind them that it is by their will that they will begin to pray out in tongues. The Holy Spirit will give the words to say, when we open our mouth and begin to speak. Instruct them not to panic, but to relax and begin to speak out words. Simple encouragement will often inspire the person to begin to pray out.

At this point, if they are still not praying in other tongues, show them the passage in I Corinthians 14:14-15 where it says that it is an act of our will. Confirm that they understand that it is their choice and involves using their own mouth and vocal chords. Once they acknowledge that, ask them if they have any further questions. Reassure them that the Holy Spirit is our Comforter and here to help us when we do not know the words to pray or what to do.

If they still do not pray out in tongues, stop for a moment and discuss other things. Take a few moments to let them relax by asking them simple questions. Often times talking about who brought them to church, their first impressions, or something of this nature, relaxes them and makes them feel comfortable again. At this point, ask them if they would like to pray again and often times, they begin praying in other tongues right away.

Do I have to feel something to be baptized with the Holy Spirit?

People's reaction to be being filled with the Holy Spirit is different for every person. While one may feel extremely emotional throughout the process, another might be very reserved and reticent. One's feelings do not determine whether they received or not. There is not a specific way a person must act in order to receive all that the Holy Spirit has to offer. It is important that you inform the person you are ministering to this reality. Even if they do not ask you this question, the devil will eventually come to try and steal away this amazing gift by bringing doubt to their mind.

I was filled with the Holy Spirit at age 17 while standing in praise and worship at church. I was worshiping, had my hands raised and began praying in other tongues. When the worship was over and everyone sat down, I did the same.

It was not an emotional experience for me, externally. But I remember that moment as a monumental moment in my Christian faith. I have also heard many stories of people who received the Holy Spirit and it was a very emotional time for them; they wept and felt extremely touched. Their experience of receiving the Holy Spirit is not better than another's, it is simply different.

We do not base our faith on an experience of emotional highs and lows; we base our faith on the Word of God and the promises therein. The essential element in receiving the Holy Spirit is that we obey based on our will to receive the Holy Spirit and then act on that faith.

7

Children are People Too!

"One generation shall praise Your works to another, and shall declare Your mighty acts." Psalm 145:4

The Bible clearly states the importance of sharing God's goodness with the younger generations. We must work with our children to teach them the ways of God. Ministering to a child who is under the age of 12 is only slightly different than ministering to an adult. The key difference centers on the reality that you are an adult and they are a child, and therefore may misunderstand what you are communicating.

When you minister to a child, do whatever you can do to get on their level physically. This will make them feel more comfortable with you because they won't have someone towering over them. Do your best to keep them from being nervous. If they have had a negative experience with adults it could be transferred to you, and they may be apprehensive around you. Be aware of the child and his or her needs; careful not to push them to make a decision out of fear.

Let the child tell you what choices they want to make. Do not put words in their mouth or tell them what they are going to do. When a child knows they want to be born again, they will be able to tell you. We know that when we were born again, it was from the heart. Allow them to come to that same decision in their heart. Kids will often say whatever you want them to in order to make the adult happy. Remember it is important not to put words in their mouth. Let them tell you what they want, and when they do, follow the Spirit and you will know what to do.

When it comes to salvation, some people ask, *"Can a little child of four to six years old really get born again?"* The answer is, yes, it is possible. Two of my children were born again before the age of 6. Especially if a child is raised in a Christian home, they will know what they want will understand the need to accept Jesus into their heart.

One of my good friends was singing a song to her little niece one time and after a while, the little girl stopped and said, *"I wish Jesus would come and live at my house."* Her niece was only four years old at the time, but she knew she wanted Jesus. My friend quickly responded that Jesus would love to come and live at her house, and would also love to come live in her heart. The little girl became excited and asked how He would do that. My friend simply explained that all she had to do was ask Jesus to come into her heart and He would.

A child that wants Jesus will receive Him. She told her niece she would pray a short prayer with her and once she did, Jesus would live in her heart. They prayed, *"Jesus, please come into my heart."* She then asked the little girl where Jesus was and she exclaimed, *"He is in my tummy!"* Now, the child did not know all the concepts, but she knew Jesus was with her. A child who wants Jesus will receive Jesus. Don't put an age limit on children. Leave that decision for the child and the Holy Spirit.

Keep it Simple

When ministering to a child, they only need to hear two verses on salvation. Children are very trusting and accept what you tell them. Children do not need to be convinced with numerous passages, like adults often times do. Show them John 3:3, and explain that in order to see the kingdom of God, they must be born again. They need to know how to be born again, so show them Romans 10:9-10. Explain that all they need to do is believe in their heart and say with their mouth that Jesus is their Lord.

At this point, go into a very simple prayer of salvation. Children need to understand what you are trying to tell them. Using simple words is the key to making certain this happens. The prayer may be as follows, **"God I come to you in the**

name of Jesus. I believe You raised Jesus from the dead, and I confess that He is my Lord. In Jesus' name, Amen." Now, they are saved!

Children also need to be baptized in water. Explain to them that it is an outward sign of what He did in their heart. Being baptized in water should be done when they are around age twelve; at this point they fully understand the significance of their decision.

Next is the baptism of the Holy Spirit. Explain to them that God has something very special for them that is a gift for everyone who has Jesus in their heart. Briefly explain what it means to pray in a heavenly language. Rely on the Holy Spirit and do not push the child into making a decision they do not understand; they need to be ready and willing to receive.

There are two main problems adults face when working with children on being filled with the Holy Spirit. The first problem is adults pushing young children to do something they do not understand and are not ready for. I heard a story about a little girl who was pressured into praying in tongues. Her parents thought they should tell her that she could do it, and told her this over and over again. The child was nervous and never spoke up. Several years later, she finally told her mom that she had thought God was mad at her and had been since she was five years old, because she couldn't pray in tongues.

We must be extremely careful and sensitive to the Holy Spirit. Children know when they are ready to receive and they will tell you. The little girl was freed from that fear of believing God was mad at her. Shortly after she told her mom of her fears, she was filled with the Holy Spirit and began praying in other tongues.

Another issue we, as adults, need to remember is that we do not belittle a child's understanding of God, and the Holy Spirit. There is not an age limit on when a child should, or shouldn't, receive the Holy Spirit. When my daughter was six years old, she called me into her bedroom and said she was ready to be filled with the Holy Spirit. We sat on the floor in her room and prayed for the Holy Spirit to come into her life, and together, we prayed in tongues. She knew exactly what she wanted and knew she was ready to receive.

With children, just like adults, you must make sure they can tell you how they got born again. Be patient in fully understanding exactly how they were born again. Once you know they have received salvation, you may proceed on to the steps of being filled with the Holy Spirit. Read them Acts 1:8 where it says: ***"But you shall receive power when the Holy Spirit has come upon you; and you shall be witnesses to Me*** *in Jerusalem, and in all Judea and Samaria, and to the end of the earth."* Tell them, *"When you receive the Holy Spirit you receive power to live the Christian life."*

Read I Corinthians 14:14: *"For if I pray in a tongue, my spirit prays, but my understanding is unfruitful."* Explain that they must decide to pray in tongues and they must use their mouth to do it. The Holy Spirit will always be there to help, but it is an act of their will; He will not pray for them. Tell them that when they were born again, they received a heavenly Father who wants to give them amazing gifts and bless their life. Their heavenly Father wants to bless them with the gift of the Holy Spirit, all they have to do is ask (Luke 11:13). Now, lead them in prayer: *"Father, in Jesus' name, I ask you for the gift of the Holy Spirit with the evidence of speaking in tongues. I will now speak in tongues in Jesus' name."* Then start praying in the Spirit, and they will, too.

It is important to explain to them the doubts and confusion that they will feel in the near future. Just as adults are attacked by the devil, he will also try to come to their minds and confuse them with thoughts of doubts and uncertainties. Remind them in Luke 11:13, God said He would give them the Holy Spirit if they asked Him. Explain that regardless of the doubts they feel, praying in tongues was real and they are filled with the Holy Spirit. Tell them that anytime they have doubts and fears, they can tell the devil to GO AWAY in Jesus' name, and he will leave.

Let them know they should pray in tongues every single day, and that they need to be with others who pray in tongues, as well. Read Jude 20: *"But you, beloved, building yourselves up on your most holy faith, praying in the Holy Spirit."* The Holy Spirit is our helper Who builds us up and makes us strong as Christians.

Keep everything simple when explaining things of salvation and the Holy Spirit to a child. They will be excited to make the right choices for God and for His Kingdom!

8
You are Able!

Minister from the Spirit

The Holy Spirit is our greatest help when we are ministering to others. For you to be the kind of witness that God desires for you to be, you must operate from your spirit, and express His life to the person you are helping. Have confidence in God's Word and what it says about being born again and filled with the Holy Spirit. As you gain confidence, you will release it in the way you communicate, and people you are ministering to will be persuaded by your excitement. Speak with authority and authenticity and know that the way Jesus spoke is our model.

It is the Spirit of God who adds life to the scriptures. Many people know and can quote John 3:16: ***"For God so loved the world that He gave His only begotten Son, that whoever believes in Him should not perish but have everlasting life."*** But unless you share that verse from your spirit, it will not have the desired effect. That verse carries the power to save the entire world, if you give it in the Spirit.

The only way you can minister from the Spirit to someone is to forget about yourself. We must not be consumed with thoughts of ourselves, but concentrate on the one we are ministering to. Focus on the person's needs and how you have the answer that will change their eternal destiny.

Remember that you are the one the Holy Spirit brought forth into that person's life to help them. They are looking for answers and direction and you are the one who is able to provide them with what they have been searching for. If you will speak to them in confidence, and give them all the love that is within you, you will be able to help them and lead them easily to salvation, and the baptism of the Holy Spirit.

God has made you able through the power of the Holy Spirit. You are able to be His witness, and He has given you His Word. As you make the decision to use the Word of God to meet the needs of the people, you will be blessed far beyond what you could ever ask or think.

God has chosen you; He has authorized and enabled you to share His love with this world. Be the bold witness you were created to be, and together we will win this world for Jesus, WON BY ONE!

For more information, booking inquiries and teaching materials by
Casey and Wendy Treat contact us at:
Christian Faith Center
33645 20th Ave S.
Federal Way, WA 98003
(253) 943-2400

Or visit our web sites at www.caseytreat.com or www.wendytreat.com